Puti/White

PATRIA RIVERA

And the bird that flew away last winter
with a broken wing
the shelter of life,
and the young woman who left to play
with the dogteeth of summer
and the soul which screeching sought the lower world
and the country like a large plane-leaf swept along
by the torrent of the sun
with the ancient monuments and the contemporary sorrow.

George Seferis, from "The King of Asine"

Frontenac House
Calgary, Al

Book and cover design: Epix Design
Cover art: Melanya Liwanag Aguila
Author photo: Joe Rivera

Library and Archives Canada Cataloguing in Publication

Rivera, Patria
        Puti/white / Patria Rivera.

Poems.
ISBN 0-9732380-9-7

        I. Title. II. Title: Puti white.

PS8635.I943P88 2005   C811'.6   C2005-900351-0

We acknowledge the support of the Canada Council for the Arts which last year invested $20.3 million in writing and publishing throughout Canada. We also acknowledge the support of The Alberta Foundation for the Arts.

Canada Council   Conseil des Arts
for the Arts   du Canada

Alberta Foundation for the Arts

Printed and bound in Canada
Published by Frontenac House Ltd.
1138 Frontenac Avenue S.W.
Calgary, Alberta, T2T 1B6, Canada
Tel: 403-245-2491   Fax: 403-245-2380
editor@frontenachouse.com   www.frontenachouse.com

1 2 3 4 5 6 7 8 9 09 08 07 06 05

Available @ ARKIPELAGO Books
1010 Mission Street
San Francisco, CA 94103 USA
www.arkipelagobooks.com

Puti/White explores the past in places buried under layers of shifting reality. Here a poet searches for her lost roots – partly remembered, partly imagined – where language questions the everyday and probes the persistent difficulties of preserving the personal from the pull of the public world. These poems seek to capture the voices that lie within, those engagements of the particular with the universal that spark moments of grace.

For Joe Rivera
and Jenny, Kim, Isobel and Rani Rivera

Acknowledgements

Much thanks for their encouragement to the people who have shown me how to find the true line: Helen Humphreys, who believed and had faith I could pursue it; Gerry Shikatani, through the Writers' Union of Canada mentoring program; Don Domanski, through the Banff Centre for the Arts Wired Writing Program; David Donnell and Michael Redhill, through the University of Toronto Continuing Education Poetry Program; Ruth Roach Pierson, for friendship, numerous kindnesses and writerly advice; my fellow writers Rosemary Blake, Sue Chenette, Maureen Harris, Kerri Huffman, Maureen Hynes, John Oughton, Julie Roorda, Norma Rowen, Mary Lou Soutar-Hynes, and Sheila Stewart; Ken Babstock and Rhea Tregebov, for commenting on the manuscript; and Winnie Quinn, for coffee and cheer.

Thanks as well to the Writers Union of Canada for opening the door by organizing the 1994 Writers of Colour Conference in Vancouver; and to Brick Books, *ARC: Canada's National Poetry Magazine*, and *The Southeast Asian Review*, for Writers' Reserve grants funded by the Ontario Arts Council.

Acknowledgement is made to the following publications and e-magazine for poems that originally appeared in them:
Fireweed: Cold War, 1957; Living on the borders,
    dying in the margins; Mother's gift
Variety Crossing: Old woman at the well; White cliffs of Dover
Six from the Sixth: A foot in Hamburg; Burnham Park,
    Philippines, 1973; Sagada mountains
Existere: 13 blossoms in a Minnesota museum
Our Own Voice: G.E. radio; Naomi in a shoebox.

And deep indebtedness to my late parents Jose Cabatuando Sr. and Petra Abes for the memories.

Contents

3   Beyond appearances

1 Women descended from birds

13 blossoms in a Minnesota museum

This one is for the books
Two chrysanthemums, two lotuses, two roses,
two peonies, a pomegranate flower,
two hibiscus, two camellias,
ling-chi signs of immortality
weaving seasons in a landscape:

Ming Dynasty. Yung-lo period. 1403-1424. Dish.
Porcelain with deep blue open clear glaze.
Lilies bouquet in bud,
full bloom, leaves on slender stems,
seed pods, arrowhead leaf, millet stem,
rush leaves tied together with swirling ribbons.

1987: the summer we arrive with hammers,
wrenches, screwdrivers, pliers, suitcases,
and a perfect heart in woodcut.

What we offer you: persimmons
of the orangest hue, rain running
like a threnody, the hard-sleeping enviers of desire,
the invention of holding hands, a seminar on the heart.

In the dark, Jim Dine defines his dictionary of self
with heart, robes, hands, skulls, tools,
Venuses, trees and flowers.
"This line comes
from the line in my heart to my head."
Around us, the eyes, the ayes, the bodies of others
in a hurry to be there.

Naomi in a shoebox

Dusk, and coming home,
we shook off the mud from our toes,
the dust of play from our legs.
Inside the house people talked
in low voices. Mother was back
from the hospital, bringing
you home, Naomi, in a shoebox.

           You were so small I
could barely
see your toes. Your fingers curled,
your lips blue and unmoving.
I waited for you to smile,
but you kept your eyes closed, even as
they lined
Father's shoebox with Mother's old lace.

They said you had to wait
for another bed of pinewood
because it was too late in the night.

I guess I must have fallen asleep.
When I woke up you were gone,
and Mother's old lace
was back on the altar with a lit candle.

What about me

And the moon said   write about me   what about me
And what did the girl with the red red red shoes
Playing with her doll
Sitting on a curb in the parking lot say
To her granny smoking beside her   head tilted back   thinking away
Or to the buzzards pecking at a lump of musty rice
Their diet of worms
Behind the library it is past noon   the sky's the colour of dust
No sun
To tell them mealtimes   they eat whenever
There's grub on the ground
They don't care about the garage sale in progress
On the walk behind the apartment buildings   old bags
Clothes   toys
Mayhem on patches of brown grass   a young girl gushes
Over a basket of Barbies   make a wish girl   make a wish
A woman rests outside the mall with her bag of chips
After a morning
Of grocery shopping   she's colour-coordinated in her turquoise shirt
On turquoise skirt looping around her thick hips enormous legs
A parachute landing on so many folds
Of flesh while the old man in the supermarket checkout counter
Gives a tip   eyes open and closed   Chockeye tuna's on sale

1945

Mother carried you in her belly
running from enemy fire.

For your birthday, she picked
                a day in the calendar –
                        a day in March –
                in between the rice fields
and the mountains of Pinaglagarian.

She remembers carrying you
                        six, seven months...

Didn't you know there was a war?

Each day she prayed
                you'd be as strong
            as the mountains they'd fled to,
feet rooted on the ground,
            as full of fire as the night flames
                    that gave them cover.

                On rainy days
she must have foraged
            the rice paddies
                    for snails and frogs:
you plucked at the knots of your brain,
                    dragged a cloak in your throat,
couldn't speak 'til you were six,
            had a hard time telling your left foot
                    from your right.

                Oh, how you loved to sleep in stairwells,
even after falling many times,
            always dreaming of cowboys,
                    the gut of ropes and guns,
what the sun holds up close,
            the thump of drums and horses.

G.E. radio

This is the house Father built
on the edge of our small town.
A wooden house with a thatched roof
and nipa shingles all around.

I liked to slide on the cool bamboo slats
and peek under my mom's loose skirt.
She didn't mind two tiny eyes
poking between her two fat legs.

At four, I waited
for the little men and women
who sang G.I. songs
and lived inside our G.E. radio.
Once, I ripped the radio's cardboard back
to see my little friends,
but all I saw were bulbous tubes
and copper wires glistening in the dark.

        I searched in all the corners,
fearing they must have slipped out,
thought they hid in the telephone by day
and came out every night.

Sitting down for tea
with the First Lady, 1954

The sepia photo captures my mother
in her one-and-only favourite frock – palm-frond
silk shift with a shirr of chiffon draping
the bodice – while the other women, artfully made up
in their pompadour hairdos, smart city clothes,
smile widely for the cameras.
> An afternoon tea with the First Lady
> on her first visit to a rice-farming town
> in the plains of Nueva Ecija.

The woman in the picture wants to disappear
into her shadow: she has never drunk
tea except to sip salabat with rice cake.
It is much too hot for an afternoon
of empty talk. Had they let her, she would've
stayed by the river to finish the day's wash,
scrubbed off the day's grime,
the full torment of strange faces,
with her work-scabbed hands.
But the presidential aides hustled her off
to the municipio to keep company
with the President's wife. Photo opportunity,
El Presidente, recently proclaimed "Man
of the Masses," knows how important
appearances can be: *The First Lady spends
an afternoon with the local mayor's wife.*
> She wouldn't let on how she survived the day,
how the sour camias soaked in burnt sugar
went with the well-coiffed ladies and their two-toned nails.
She grips a Spanish fan, a memento from her abuela.
She appears tight and vestal, her thin lips feigning a smile.

Erasures

I dream of doors and labyrinths, enclosures,
old houses fronting ancient cemeteries,
of pilgrim aunts and uncles leaving earth,
a huffle of voices.
Uncles anchored in their camisa chinos,
aunts passing in flowing panuelos.
We buried them long ago,
yet they stride in a camber of light,
faces scumbled for a final exposure
of all the good lies they'd told:
Aunt Ursula, who died of T.B.
in the city sanatorium, married to Uncle Paco
who spat blood in the cuspidor,
Uncle Peping, lord of the town casino,
and husband of silent Aunt Maria – they all joined the others.
Aunt Aurelia, second youngest of seven sisters,
ignored her spouse on her deathbed,
called on all the saints except her husband's namesake.
Aunt Pascuala forgave her man, Uncle Deo, thank God,
even though he kept a mistress in the next town.
And our double-barrelled Aunt Nicasia
who opened her hearth to childhood summers,
taught us how to wash clothes by the riverbed,
served us plump tomatoes and fried smoked fish.
Tales of relations and conjugations,
afterimages opening and closing.

Women descended from birds

Maria. Petra. Nicasia. Pascuala. Maxima. Aurelia. Ursula.

Aves: The surname of the dead.

Seven sisters, the seven stars of the skies,
all descended from the birds –
the mayas, the crows, the sparrows of Penaranda.
They farmed along burnt hills,
panned gold dust from brooks and streams,
waited for monsoon rains to fill the rice paddies.

In summer they scoured clams and shrimps from the riverbed,
               dug mudfish from abandoned wells,
picked betel nuts and ikmo leaves twining round palm trees,
                    broiled locusts for supper,
gathered ripe duhat, green mangoes and sineguelas
          from ancestral orchards.

In May before the harvest, they threaded sampaguita
and ylang-ylang, flower-of-flower, into boughs and garlands
for the Virgen de los Remedios.
               Each tore a hundred petals of exultation,
          prayed for good husbands.

               What they made of their lives –
the odds and hopes of their existence, the long histories
of their wifely devotions – they had no time to speak of this.
          You take what you will, they said:
the shadows and the light, the presence in the absence.

Cold wave

Aunt Ursula weaned us from twirling
our hair in katuray twigs, the aunt who went
to beauty culture school to learn how
to lacquer nails in moon shapes. She lined
her brows in high thin pencil arcs,
painted a fan of colours on the tiny space
above her eyes. To us who lived each day in amazement,
she was our homecoming queen,
the one who went away,
the one who took the world, its textures and shapes,
brought it back in a box
of rubber and plastic curlers,
neutralizers, chemicals that bobbed our hair
in a permanent wave.

Soon we grew, and her many suitors pared down
to the suitable one, the farmer she married and had many
children with. She thought she would live her life
like the stories she read,
like those who've inherited the earth,
not a litany of hard times when the farms didn't yield
enough for farmwives to have their hair curled.
She plodded on, but the shiver of a plague came
and took her in a swelling heave.
My aunt wasted away –
fast, as if pressing the edges of her life
would allow the wave of cold comfort
to follow her world's short drift.

The scent of mangoes on a lazy afternoon

On the verge of a summer solstice
bunched green rice stalks
point arrows of precipitation
from streams that shoulder out the river;
        tilt and shift of wet slate
river rock

hover of sulphur in an orange afternoon
resined breath of Grand-Aunt Ela
hatching mangoes golding under a bed
warmed by bodies of callow women
        their rumps of sorrow
penance for barrenness of bedrock
        precipitous mass
seeding the everyday corners of the day.

Silence levels the dark
birdnip and tuck of small hours
hide my forebears' flagrant predilection
for warm musk of ripeness
quick-scatter of tears
while they wait solemn as bats for their quarry.

Cold War, 1957

Manila, Philippines

Before we knew how to spell "desk,"
Teacher taught us to duck under one.
Better yet, at the sound of three bell rings,
to line up and down the staircase,
out onto the schoolyard
to hug the ground under the banaba trees.

We waited for the H-bomb,
the egg from the sky,
the parachutes
from Mainland China.
We waited for the invasion,
Red soldiers in their
full regalia.
                    As we lay there on the grassy mound,
red ants crept up our shins,
leaving prickly bites.
After so many drills
we came to love the smell of moist earth
and freshly cut grass
on our sweaty shirts.
                    Sometimes,
we turned over and watched
a congregation of butterflies
sob into the branches,
then spring free from the banaba trees.

Geography class, 1960

We roamed streets we first drew in Grade 4
learning the topography of monsoons.

La Loma,
our barrio, grew like a lichen on the foothills
of Sierra Madre Mountains. The Second World War
scorched its brown knolls into a suburb
of Manila's illustrious dead, made even more
infamous by a huge cockpit, and pigs skewered
on bamboo spits, roasted for everyone's celebrations.

Cocks and crows, pitogo trees and banyan roots
scuffed shadows on aureoled tombs, bloated urns,
crosses, sandstone angels, shrivelled maggots,
mausoleums, crypts piled on top of one another.
The scent of frangipani trailed humid evenings.

After the war, American soldiers decamped,
left us their Quonset huts, their taste for PX goods.

We did not bury our dead here.
They would've felt strange in this city of niches
and clapboard houses. The betting in the cockpit
would've drowned all grief:
Sa pula, sa puti –
the red and white cockfights crowing our luckless lives,
my aunts' wailing – erased the small consolation
of a sky always blue.

Bellas

Ubi amor, ibi oculus. St. Thomas Aquinas

Before it became the Bethany Baptist Church
it had been a rice silo. Before that, a moviehouse.
And way, way before, when the trains passed through
Penaranda, in the years after the war when local business
was booming and they were building the hydro dam
to catch the water from the mountains, it was,
what Mother used to call a house of ill repute.
Those honky-tonk women who fleeced the farmers
and the dam workers of their hard-earned money
were ba-a-a-a-d, so bad my mother made the sign
of the cross every time she mentioned them. Those women,
Susmaryosep! My cousins and I would have been
cursed to hell like those men had my mother known
that at harvest time, after moonlit games of kick-the-can,
we crossed the street and crawled behind the santan bushes
to spy inside that big house and its many little rooms.
With a roll of cheap tickets, a farmer could dance
the whole night through, drink his sorrows away,
forget he had a wife and twelve kids. How we envied
those women their bright, flouncy dresses,
fake pearls, long, red nails. To dance and be paid for it –
to us, it beat being in the cowboy movies.
As my boy-cousins herded us through the dark
scented nooks, we groped among curtains,
awed by the narrow beds, shadows of linked bodies.
Neither angels nor beasts, we wondered what to call them.
Shapes of guilt and desire, was this what love is?

Puti

If he hadn't been so thin, I would have imagined him
as the young man who took the leading lady into
the sunset, out of the dark, cavernous stage of Liz Theatre.
This was the late '50s, and in my nine-year-old mind's eye,
his pale white skin, dirt-blond hair, tall nose
cut him above the other guys in our shantytown.
He never played with the neighbourhood gang.
His aunts, Creole women from Zamboanga, spoke English
and Chabacano. We never saw his mama or papa.
Thought he came with the Reparations goods,
with the cheese and dried milk served at school recess.
I had always dreamt of war. Bazookas and bayonets.
Human bodies as fodder for cannons. In the *Readers' Digest*
I saw his relatives, and stories and pictures of "Life in These
United States."
Was his father one of those guys in "Humor in Uniform"?
In my dream, salvation came in a barrel of green apples,
hoarded up Mt. Arayat, snow falling on the Quonset huts of
Clark Air Base.
If he knew where he came from, it must have caused him
a lot of grief. My mother once said,
"Beware of boys who can't look at you in the eye."
          My white boy, he had a sideways glance. His flinty
eyes darted when he spoke. It was as if he didn't want you
to capture their moment, like a bird that'd feed off your palm
but fly at a moment's notice. He got into scrapes, robbed
people's homes, was jailed for many hold-ups and petty thievery.
He was in and out of jail. He was on the edge of something
darker than he knew.

O to Bambang we go

Next to Divisoria market, it is the best place
to go to for lace – bundles and bundles
of it cased in cords, taffeta – lace
scalloping the world from end to end,
oddments of handbags from the '50s, unused:
velvet and velveteen, bottle-green shape
remnants of Picasso squares, hexagons, spheroids
– and thick, grey, woollen dresses and skirts to keep
buns covered in 43 degrees Celsius. And for under-
garments, bolts of Kentucky poultry feed bags
printed with flowers of cotton fields, maize-yellow
panties sewn from huge flour sacks from Minnesota,
soaked for three days in kerosene to wash away the paint –
O the Stateside feel of it, on salty, brown skin.

Watching television through a wire mesh fence

On Friday nights after school we'd hie off to a grassy lot
beside the rich man's house, set up wooden stools outside
the wire mesh fence. We'd watch Lassie and Lucy and Desi,

but most especially John Wayne lassoing bandits
and dumping them into the OK Corral. We never understood
their words, we didn't speak English, but we sighed

and gawped at those wondrous manes, marvelled at
those huge horses galloping into our dreams. Mosquitoes feasted
on our grubby thighs, bore their hunger into our marrow.

On starry nights, we forgot our milk-can games by the moon,
forsook patintero for evenings that paraded endless cowboys
and dogs saving children from snowstorms or the ice-thaw.

We crooned with Bing and dreamt of White Christmases,
of chestnuts roasting on an open fire, when back home,
small dried fish, most likely, sat by the wood stove.

We watched behind the backs of the rich man's sons and
daughters in their warm chesterfield, oblivious of the eyes
that saw through thin wire holes. Then one Friday noon

a concrete wall stood where once a wire mesh fence gave us
passage into a world shorn of sweltering heat, a world bathed in
the soft light of snowdrifts and apple blossoms.

Mother's gift

From the old jewelry cabinet
remove the violin pin, the butterfly brooch,
the pearl studs, Grandmother's emerald ring.
Tuck them into tiny gunnysacks
and roll them into the crevices
of worm-eaten posts.

It is late morning
in Mother's house.
From her garden
she has dug out
a handful of yellowed evergreens.

Labrador tea?

She wouldn't say,
only proffers her gift:
a clump of gnarled, serrated leaves,
bushy stems tauped by sun,
and fuzzy roots still damp with earth.
All her world,
her ideas of it,
all her doubts
and affirmations.

Flagellants

It is the year presumably when the Black Nazarene
decides to take a walk,
instead of carrying his cross in the back of a truck,
leaving devotees to put their cat-o'-nine-tails
and bruises in the sun-dried-tomato landscape till the last hour.
In the call for simplicity,
they will seek intercession,
protection from injury and misfortune as usual,
forego the mustard-maroon
cloaks and fake-gold crucifixes and medallions
for the midnight blue of solemn vows,
penances, mortifications.
Supplicants will cry on the dot,
ask for deliverance
from death, incurable disease – more healing,
their votive candles lighted to flutter
guttered devotions to the grief and agonies of their faith.
In the reredo of the baroque altar,
old women will slip prayers of veneration
to their favoured saints, each hole articulating
their wish, profound sentiment,
to the hooded figures in wood and terracotta.
And this being the season of Lent,
a time of spareness, fasting and abstention,
the pastor's assistant will keep the many-faceted cruets
in the vaults, tuck away the layered crinolines and brocades
in mothballs, empty the rectory's drawers of buntinged hopes.

Wake

When our neighbour,
      the jeepney driver,
died, his family couldn't cough
      up enough money for a proper
wake. Instead, they lit candles
      and stuck them on four
empty milk cans to light the corners
      of the pallet where he lay.
On top of his closed eyes
      they put a coin
each, to pay the boat guide
      should his soul reach
the other side of the river.

Sister home for the weekend

When she came home she did not say a word
                for a very long time.
                The hours went by the tick of the lizards.
The holes in her eyes wouldn't leave us.
                Barricades, poor wages, backbreaking work,
the women in the garment factory hurling their lunch pails
                at phalanxes of soldiers on the picket line,
the men beaten up, fired at like woodpigeons in a carnival.

Now when she jerks her hand to reach out to us,
her scarred knuckles coil, grey as her argument, marked
                    where cigarette butts
            had tattooed targets on a mesh of veins.
                    Under her skirt, they stuck a live cord,
ran current enough to light the bulb in her cell,
            the blurred plot of her coded life,
her questioners getting edgier with each turn.

Big dreams

Fifteen and hawking boiled ducks' eggs along the tracks,
a young man kept big dreams,
kept his mother's songs in his breast,
kept her words from the seven drunken men
who accosted him at the rail crossings
demanding seven boiled eggs for seven guardian angels.
He refused, they taunted and attacked him.

In the hospital the doctor said the youth was punched
and kicked,
his chest slashed with a fan knife, his body pinioned to the ties
left to be run over by the local train.

When he came to, his legs were hanging by their skin,
had to be cut off,
one below, the other, above the knee.

He said he'd promised his mother
and brothers and sisters back in the paddy fields:
a house and a little farm, not duck's eggs.

Old woman at the well

It was a sign of progress,
                    this artesian well
brought in by the Reparations Bill.
            Potable water for the small, dried-up hamlet,
not rainwater caught in drums
nor shallow in ground pumps
nor piped through dried-up mountain crevices.
            This water would be good enough
to go with morning, noon and evening meals.
                        Water worth the wait
for barrio folk lining up from sun-up to sundown.

Resourceful middle-aged women,
mothers with young children,
waited for the overflow –
            when in between pourings,
            water was collected into a huge vat,
            for washing dirty clothes,
            for scrubbing unwashed children.

The week before the well's inauguration,
the lines of waiting women and children swelled,
            the project yet to be finished,
            the concrete yet to be poured,
            the gears engaged.
The work crew proceeded with the test-run,
            opening the spigot full blast,
                        letting the water gush,
carefully saved in tin pails, buckets, basins.

By late noon, the sun had hidden behind a cloud.
The line-up, too, seemed to thin
                as an old woman with a bucket
took her turn at the spout. She barely noticed
            her loose, long hair catch the spokes
                    of the waterwheel, pry the secret out
            of her scalp.

Dogteeth

We did not know then
how to care for those we love.
Now we give them a bowl of bones
and water,
at intervals.
We tether them close
to home,
guard them as they guard
us, who always crave for
affection we can neither give
nor take.
We define them as they defy us.

What the wind catches

In the end there were not enough bed sheets
to tie one to the other to allow her bony legs to reach
the ledge of the apartments below.
She did not have time to look
down the steep incline where pedestrians
and cars, storefront windows, and revolving
doors cast spiky shadows on the streets.
If she had, she might have stopped in her tracks, bearing gifts
to the watchtower clock, collecting impressions,
burnished images, sounds of her daily drudge:
the stains in the urinal, the muck on the walls,
phlegm drip-dried on ancient damasks.
She could have slogged on were it not
for those late nights in that bed next to the window,
the wolf hunting her numb body,
fear etching leaves of mimosa on the walls
(those pinnate tips she teased as a child),
all that she'd fought for
draining into the cracks, all her history sifting –
sifting quietly through the dark,
and the world around her drawing back. As she plunged
deeper, she tried to snatch onto the rope of the steel
flagpole, felt her weight pull her down ten storeys
into the windless streets.

Burnham Park, Philippines 1973

I followed the bloodstains on the grass,
the sidewalks and pathways of Burnham Park.

Early morning, the workers hadn't gone out yet,
even the peanut sellers and the fruit vendors were still

asleep. The crimson stains left not splatters,
but tiny drops, on blades of undulant green,

rolled-in twisted clumps, love-lies-bleeding in the shadows
of agonic fall-as-they-may inky red spots, caterwaul

of cats in heat, slight breeze leaving a trail of cat's paws
on the manmade pond, murky with the mud of summer.

Here, V.'s mother lay splayed among
this grove of wet pines, eyes to the sky, her hacked back

suppurating onto the crabgrass, feeding the fungi.

Divinations

Let our gods perceive the ruminations of distance, where
Mercies untangle the light of the moon's drawl.

Perhaps the cerements of tea leaves will wrap the rhythms and
Tones of people's riddled silences through subterranean fugues.

Yet, patience. Scatter the bones of the dead. Their feathery veins
Will augur the hard future of memory, the almanac of betrayals,

What we fear to touch, the astonishing fields of horror and
Shame. search for the peaks of throbbing hearts,

Seize the hallowed monstrance cupping testimonies
Of unworthiness, hiding the cryptography of lies.

Sagada mountains

Green is the colour of morning:
a young woman brushing her hair,
posed on a stool on top of the wood table
in an old house in Sagada mountains.
I cannot see her face, she's swung her head back.
I will forever imagine
how her face must have looked
up close, what stories you told her
to fill the silence on long walks
up the trail where the mountains
bled green with foliage,
how you kept those days sacral
in the folds of myth, humdrum rituals,
why I believed you, why her memory
skims through the bamboo slats
where light escapes.

2 The geography outside

Living on the borders, dying in the margins

Attending the wake of a woman I've never met,
                      I joined in the prayers –
waiting to pay my respects.
           Ave Maria purisima…

An old woman who died alone in her bed.
        The pidgin Latin segueing into my native tongue…
           Aba ginoong Maria, napupuno ka ng grasya…

I lost track, couldn't find the words
      to link the chain, the litany of prayers –
         Hail Mary, full of grace…
In ten years I have lost
    the words that would bridge
        my foreign self to the past.
Just because my daughters' teachers said:
        Speak to them in English, always,
           from dawn when they wake up
              to dusk before they sleep.

Rock them to the sounds of English,
spoken, heard and read.

A friend, exiled down south,
    has taught her daughters the new language.
      She writes: One cannot escape the net
      that keeps the vanquished in bondage.

At home, my daughters scream,
      I lash out in another tongue.
    Somehow the words do not seem to match
      the nettles that lacerate and I roil inside
because I cannot put words to my anger,
    because they are always waiting for me to fumble.
I cannot even get mad and not get stuck
      in the idiom, the syntax,
    the tenses, the grammar

because I think in my native tongue first –
                bayan, pag-ibig sa tinubuang lupa –
      nouns, verbs, adjectives
                    only to get lost in the prepositions,
      the gerunds, the appositives.

The old woman in her pink casket –
                did she think in my native tongue too?
      Did she dream foreign words would give
                      meaning to her life?
      The litany of prayers –
      strains as familiar as my mother's incantations
                Tore ni David, toreng garing...
weave in and out
                exorcising the air
                in this room full of flowers and candles,
      flowers and languages without a scent.

The opacity of pebbles

We flew in to Warsaw then to a small northern town in Poland,
to see the sights – hills, mountains, rocks, and farmers returning
from the fields – also, to investigate the opacity of pebbles.
In nearby Szetejnie, in old Lithuania, we left the poet drinking
kvas from a tin cup, felt the flesh of the calamus march up and
down our throats riding the one-horse britzka. The poet pointed
to a boulder where once stood the village of Peiksva and to the
hare that once was and was pointed at by a young man
also now gone. Workers danced the tango in the moon glow,
and in a textile factory, an inventive man found a better way of
dyeing batik, not by crushing the fabric with feet and a pebble,
but with feet and many pebbles, the perfectibility of letting
pebbles grind colours in rivulets from fabric onto running
streams. Before I knew it, I was five months pregnant, carrying
this baby to workers' meetings, getting furious at the lost hours,
and missing my flights twice. How can I suffer so much
anguish, forget to change my flight schedule when I should
have known, I've been to Poland and back, seen my friend's
hometown, the workers dancing in the park?

Three images

1 [Bribes]

Five, you must have been five, howling for a fake ring
that the dentist earlier gave your sister.
        You didn't know such bribes are sometimes made
           to make life a little easier.

On the front page of today's paper, in the dentist's office,
          others are not as fortunate.
Like the man who poured gasoline on his own body
to make a statement to the world. Anything
      but this – living in a foreign land
while wife, son and daughter
hide in fear in abandoned houses.

Or the middle-aged woman who was run over
by her enraged husband.
              Twice because,
      as he says, she deserved it.

And as you play
hide-and-seek by the door,
you, with the cherub cheeks and pure eyes,
will only remember the joy
of a mottled-green rock encrusted
in fake gold
encircling your pink, stubby fingers.

2 [Into my daughter's footsteps]

Deep freeze covers the roadside,
the old pathway winding down John Street.
A storm spiral heaps white chaff, a foot deep,
onto the frozen ground.

                              Crossing the curb,
on the stretch that leads to home,
my daughter, third of four, hefty,
presses huge footprints (not angel's wings)
into the snow bank.

3 [Horses crossing Davisville walk bridge]

December's mauve dusk.
                          Above
               the rail tracks,
                  drifts of snow clot tree branches,
encase tombs, crosses, broken angels
                       in the old cemetery.
As the train passes, chortles of conversations,
                  occasional laughter.
                       Up there,
            on a narrow bridge too skimpy for cars,
a pack of dark iron
                 mares bridle, waiting for
             the cortege, carrying bodies to be buried.

The geography outside

Leave them the invisible chances of those circumstances,
the contradictions, the muddy paths of the slack-jawed,
the convolutions, the slow run between the bends of the two
roads twirling the map of imagination.
They slide past a tumult of grass.
If she had some advantages, many times she would have saved
human warmth like yeast gathering on the wrong moment,
the solemn pastures of the evanescing shadow. All she could
give was a stubborn figment of a confession barely clawing at
the truth, knowing she was not capable of a lie. It was a grace
she brought, like a quickness of temper in the wrong places, an
amazing knowledge of the possible. In the dim light, she left a
furtive slip, a trail of dust whispers that could only happen in
some fast-tracked movie on the dry-stone wall, among the sedge
and tall grass, "This way – this was where it happened."

Full particulars

1

          Let the day begin. Let me hang on
                    to days which may not come back.
Let me enjamb into memory every speckle
          of mist or skein of clouds, every rooftop
                         jutting from the valley, every trace of tree
from east to west, even the lake's smooth line,
          imperceptible in the nebulous warp of night
                    washing off its sins in the weft of the morning.

2

Structure is what you wanted:
        a framework for our lives that prefigures
           · completion, a hermeneutic desire
for clean lines of beginning, middle, end.

Everything's here for a reason: the here, the now,
the yet-to-be.
      I live for the thick moment, want to capture
      all of my life. Here's to
      the penultimate quartz ticking the pulse of the universe!

3

First memory: a curiosity for the obvious,
             what's behind objects, what's behind desires.

I lie on the shiny bamboo slats of our nipa house,
face up to the world, wanting to investigate the darkness
of my mother's womb, peeking under her skirt
          as she walks to the kitchen and back.
                              Nada.
I wait and wait and sleep.

My older brother, back from a school day, vertiginous,
          runs a fever, hallucinates, harbours a caterpillar on his leg,
sees apparitions, elves, gnomes, in every nook.
          The village herb doctor says, "Namatanda," spooked,
and prescribes herbs, grass, twigs. My brother
heals, becomes an M.D., serves in 'Nam,
is mugged in the Bronx, moves to a three-acre estate
in Pittsburgh, and dies of a heart attack.

My mother lives through her eight full-terms,
six stillbirths, including Naomi, my sister,
they buried in a shoebox.
                    My other brother, he was seventeen
when he started to draw twirls, whorls, zigzags,
all manner of windrows –
Our very own Van Gogh
who took endless jeepney rides and returned,
scoring the lizard's cunning into walls.
A preemie, pitong buwan, the one whom everyone teased
because he was slow. Most days he was sullen,
a stubborn son whom my father described
as a man of notable reserve, an immovable eye
looking at a world he could not comprehend.

4

There are limits to what God will allow you,
Mother used to say. She stood by my younger brother
as he grew worse, visiting him
week after week up to the day he died,
not from his nightmares, but from a brain aneurysm.

Wars, earthquakes, floods, births, deaths
and our repetitive, tectonic lives
fulfilled my mother's prophecy: years of abundance
followed by years of penury. Meron, wala, meron.

5

       I have buried the past so deep I cannot find the cicatrix
where it all began. Did it begin with the insurgents
burned at the stake? My great-great-grandfather's patch
of land in Pinaglagarian, where wild rice grew on the slopes
until the hills eroded from years of slash-and-burn?
       I have no memories, only heard stories
of deeded land turned over to the authorities
because my illiterate forebears could only trace an X
to mark their names.

Years later, whoever spoke for the peasants and the workers
was declared a dissident, packed off to prison camp. We buried
words under the frangipani trees.
Silence seared the circumference of the poblacion,
spread into the streets, scorched the mouths of the rivers.
The mountains were inconsolable, heavy with tears
of the disappeared.

       As we verified the truth of our lives
my friends sweated on blocks of ice, became target ducks
to army helicopters,
given the water cure with their heads shoved in toilet bowls.

Public notice: We grieve for no one in particular. "We all go on
living after the others are murdered," writes Neruda.
       Though we've made
       a safe life, we would not escape the conquerors.

6

Ten thousand miles away in this new land,
we succumb to the city's lures, pooh-pooh our pan de sal,
hanker for a mantled fireplace, the two-car garage,
money in the bank, trips to Varadero or to Acapulco,
                                        or even the fake accent,
the f– word over the cell phone to show we belong.

At the checkout counter, an old man from my hometown cocks his ear.
"Kumusta, manong?" I ask him, and he cracks the biggest grin,
wanting to hear familiar words.
        Was his the puzzled face I saw in a local paper
picking plump pumpkins on a seniors' outing to an Oshawa farm?

This night, the morning paper declares, it will be heavenly business –
                as usual. I shall carry the stones of my people,
ride along the planets of Jupiter and Saturn,
                perhaps wait for the Seven Stars
        to soar to the backwaters of the Milky Way,
                        listen to the sound of grapes falling.

When my brother wakes from his long sleep

The local acceleration of gravity
                    pushes memory into a black hole,
        pins the distance to the horizon
                        as a finite probability.
Consciousness drifts
                into the snail's grave, the fourth
        stage when mind succumbs and resists pursuit.

        My brother wakes from his long sleep,
allowed this other life where he can take care
        of his family, his wife and two daughters
                too young to have known him.

If he had checked his previous equation, would he
        have known that the outside shell
                        has an aperture
collapsing matter into infinite forms?

Hawking says if the universe contracts, the arrow
                of time would reverse and people would live their
lives backward. I wonder if, played back, time surges on a plane
                        through infinite speed.

        My niece presses all the buttons of the convection oven,
        waiting to see how it will work. The domino
                pins light up, right to the 12th dot, the knobs
sizzle in the heat.
                My brother, fancying he can swallow
light, catches the experiment in time, turns off
                the buttons. The iron grills turn cold.

A foot in Hamburg

Slow take on an afternoon in Hamburg.
The dragon lady collects
pumps in 256 colours.
A few blocks from the Reeperbahn
where the Beatles played their first German gig.
It's been reported she's never
thrown any out. A smouldering sun
sears the shops. For disco dancing
she orders a pair with flash
cubes on square heels,
wattage enough to light every slum colony
from Manila to New York. Price is not an issue.

The papery displays wallpaper seconds
and three times as many shapes
on the sidewalk, forced-blooms on paisley,
huge sun and cornflowers on the pavement.
Nearby, a carpet store lays out the last
of the summer's dark Persian rugs
and kilim of finest wool and silk.
She feels so low she stacks
and saves all her shoes.

Down the street a hearse passes
the antiquitaeten and an old shoe store
with its plate glass window
encasing bluchers and wingtips
in brown, black, white,
and the remains
of a foot
shod in a low boat.

Ancient boundaries

Lost in the intimate distance,
we talk of ancient boundaries,

the legs of space and time. We are experts
at the thoroughly bizarre, speculative, rigorous.

Wrought down by duty and inclination,
we are two candles circled by infinite suns,

embraced by a limitless void.
Nothing of what we remember remains.

Mornings wrap me in guilt

Mornings
        at Apartment 2410:
blue sky,
expanse of space reaching out,
the southwest wind beating heartaches
       on to the sunburnt windows.

            Turning right, I climbed the first hill
in disgrace, got paid for my bird imitations,
       fell onto my hands and knees. Got up, stunned,
carried the burden of my muscle spasm,
          only to stumble
       into an unhappy expression.

            I want to sleep lightly,
feel concern for the easily injured,
renounce the greed of metagods who snicker
at the silent approach of women of virtue.
       Speak. Teach.
       Write a bad cheque.

Swing a mace among the starch plants in the terrace
       into the heart of a torturer, or wrap it in twigs.
Grind your duelling swords. Preserve your thoughts in brine
          or gasoline thickener.

            Encourage the iron-bearing
chert to sing an operatic melody. Summon him
       in the likeness of a racehorse.

3 Beyond appearances

Between shorelines

**1 After viewing *Memories of Quicksand*,
sculptures by Doug Guildford**

Grains, porous, pour
through inconstant sands,
once-huge rocks broken down
by interstices of time and stone.
Animal and vegetable particles,
foliage and masts of ocean kelp
batter the shoreline,
sleep through the summer,
bake in the sun beside holes
we've dug on the beach, each one
a plastic work of defiance.

                  Whoever sweeps
the shore shall harvest a feast –
broken shells, shards of dory fish bones,
the rotten remains of a blue fin tuna,
a grapnel dragged by tides
to sift the ocean floor.

2 The last hour in May

An hour of life left in the day
as we scan white crests on choppy cold water.
Rough, dark weather batters barren domes of rock,
whalebacks for our limp tents and tired backs.
A kayak slices through the waves, slips under the wind,
sojourner seeking the last great wave.

                  O if it were infinite!
The last light recedes, the last of the Mayflies flit
round rocks and bushes, dipping, twirling, kissing
the water, swerving upwards as the sun goes down.

Caryatids

Dusk and falling light
On Precambrian rock
The mind wanders
Uproots memory
Of granite under the stars
And I weep
Independent of
The notes
You shift positions
Climb out of our hole
Wet spasms
Dry air
The unbearable pain
Of our journey
Too close
Abruptly sundered

Beyond appearances

After a poem by Mark Strand)

When the waning cold light came by the lake cracked with ice,
the white houses near the shore stood ghastly up close.
Small latticed windows appeared glowing
in the distant reaches of your frozen cabin.
Neither to desire nor to want, not to recognize the power
beyond yourself, beyond your world even, escapes me.
You who have pinioned your hopes on surfaced covenants,
imagined wishes of fallen evangels seeking solace
on the snow-blown earth. Not once did you feel
the night's glow cover the empty night even as you stopped
being.
                    Is that where you belong?
among the hidden valleys carved by ice, in the false erasures
of night wind, beyond appearances, possessed yet empty?

The weight of air

JERICHO: Sound breaking walls, *Multimedia Installation by Monica Van Asperen Museum of Modern Art, Buenos Aires, Argentina, November 2000*

Un segundo, dos segundos…

You breathe air into a bubble of indefinable weight,
line up balloons in needlespins without symmetry,
rows of blown transparent balls pinned on wires,
festooned on old concrete posts,
each one hauling a measure of your breath,
small takes at fathoming the nothing that is there,
ether, the passage of time in pure breath sounds,
the heft and weight of longing.
You say you do not know where it will lead you.
The labyrinths of breath-seconds have a life all their own:
air kissing steel, shadows of light lustrating sounds.
They scream arias, follow their intuitions,
soar into the moonrise.

Marconi listens to the holes in the ground

On December 12, 1901, Italian inventor Gugliemo Marconi received the first transatlantic wire message on Signal Hill, St. John's, Newfoundland and Labrador.

In the woods you stalk
grass   lizard   nuthatch
examine empty spaces
cracks of mounds
skeletons of calcified bushes
nests hanging from treetops
pry earth from roots
limbs from cragwood
rest your ear on crevices
wait for sounds
from moss-covered wombs
of disappearing presences
you've so much
to tell to those above-
ground   feet on precipice
if only they'd listen
to the hush
between breaths
follow the curvature
of the earth
wait for the hollow spaces
of dried sponges
to transmit invisible waves
from the yawn
of the open cave
to the ottoia worm
sleeping on its fossil bed

Remembering the word

When they came to, they were asked to keep one stone
to remember the word they would bring to their grave,
gouged in rock, written in the language of the forgotten,
dictated by time when the world knew what it was doing,
before the dimensions of distance and space unfolded
new pixels and arguments for a virtual shadow illumining
letters, skillful turns of muddied glass, the law of hands
that break: witness of the hour cutting elements of flesh
inhabiting a crystallized attention, the evasion of years
waiting for the blossom of season, the fading, perishing
old explanations of decay and longing, when hearts,
pushing, eviscerated from wounds, the lamb's blood,
the scattering branches, the crisping scratches of leaving,
the dismemberment of memory stubbornly resisting.

Jardin del Engano

Jardin del Engano: *Tecnica mixta, by Monica Millan, Centro Cultural Borges, Buenos Aires, 1999*

Impermanencia/Lagarte

Egg-of-the-earth cocoons little loves in sealed vaults
     black feelers search for endings
        crunch   gnaw   chomp leaf and bark
    rain spits on tin roof

Midnight moults the instar
   the pupa hops and screams in the impenetrable cocoon   imago
hinting the forms of fathers and mothers
    the amatory practices of moth spinning silken loop
who wrongs the disenchanted

Victoria Regia

Paradise of enchanted gardens
reticulate rough spider web patterns
       on slopes and coastal planes
    ravines   dark forest
     baroque headwaters
    surface hollows
frame the foliage
    of the humiliated and the vanished
the sheer drop of those dedicated
      to serve and build

Jardin de la Flor

Love enthralls the keeper of the garden
     a gorge of flowers
       berms   winding tracks of frog
    threading furrows
        glistening gutters of desire

On the lift and fold   of surface elevations
emptied bird's nests   excavated lies

Jardin de la Nube

Observe the canticle of ice
        filigree of snow-covered branches
                        parasol of white cloud
the sweet ambition of small mounds
                on hidden ruins
snowfall   covering corrosions
        shielding necessity

Jardin del Gusano

Walk through hedgerows   the archetypal floral borders
                a conspiracy of dreams
on rose-spattered lawns
            buttes jutting
                an espalier
                        of butterflies taking off
            sequined beds of glass beads
liana   crocheted   sutured   embroidered
                in silk thread on flesh
meadow of cryptic stones on blood trails

Black feelers unreel from the watchful
                        worm wiggling its head
            through the cave
                at the tip of the eggshell
            bites for air
                        The silk moth gives birth   dies
leaving eggs the size of a period.

If

In late winter, the early morning fog
will hide the stands of trembling aspen.
                              If you want to feel
the wind in your face, trace your steps
round the sinuous stone walls
towards a slope of old-growth trees –
beech, elm and red oak – stubborn
trunks, the lay of hills in one embrace.
It's not the end,
allow the breadth of the land to bury
your disappointments. You can
seek solace in the fit of boulders
hugging the outcrop. The bromegrass,
grey and bountiful,
can make a flat and wavy pillow,
turn your tears of mourning into many-mouthed springs.

Suspicious cargo

1 [Pretty River]

The captain alerted authorities
suspicious cargo could be aboard
his freighter plying
the Pacific Ocean.
Two hundred seventy-five containers
full of retail goods from China,
and hidden among silk cloths,
incense and candles,
eyes and ears, flesh and bones,
spilled urine, excrement.
The conditions inside were,
says Cpl. Grant Learned,
"really quite horrific."
Thirty-six stowaways,
among them six women,
crammed into two containers
for two weeks when Pretty River entered
the ports of Xing-ang, Dalian, Qingdao, Busan,
before heading for Vancouver.
When the ship docked, the waves
echoed the noise of many waters.

2 [White cliffs of Dover]

Across from Sanguette,
      the French town on the selvage
    of the English Channel,
         the rugged cliffs of Dover rise
         incandescent.
    Tracking the tonguing of tides,
the sun bursts pins
        of light on cresting waves.

    Did the men in that truck hear the hum
      of breaking furls,
the pebbles and seashells crushing on the shore?

That hot, hot summer
    the tomatoes quickly ripened in the back,
    blocking the air vent
        with their trickling juice.

In Fujian, in southeastern China,
    He-Xiaohong keeps hoping her husband
  is one of two survivors.
        Fifty-eight
  dead, huddled,
    trying to sneak into Dover.

3 [Hung Lo's diaries]

After she died, Hung Lo's daughters
took away her diaries, the dog-eared
notebooks where she scribbled notes
to herself, items she did not want to miss
when she wanted to bring back days gone:
the geology of her thoughts,
the breviary of her dreams,
not wanting to leave word shadows,
traces of a hoarfrost's regret.
She wanted the pages
to tear a tune from her heart, unravel sweet
longing, mark where she would have gone, how
she would have stitched the uncertain
patterns of her life,
burred whispers of tiny steps.

Air tap

Rumble of spat hot air down the chute of buildings connected
by common paths straddling apartment walk-ups, coffee
houses and delis serving hot drinks to newcomers with their

long dresses, children streaking out of dingy rooms into endless
green lawns. Everywhere there's a gathering of men, women
and young ones, a Georgic feast of morning sun, coffee cups

and doughnuts, all the apartment buildings connected by coffee
houses on the ground floor, tightly packed immigrants streaming
from one building to the other, passports on chairs, documents

of the disappeared duplicated, replicated, as if the hearing
officers would not mind the signs, like musical illuminations,
that the resourceful invaders will not infect people with
compromised immune systems ("We know little where

they come from, how they end up here, or even what they
are.") They've shed their genetic material and used a coiled
tube to blast their hosts' energy-generating systems ("We

are perplexed, they have done the seemingly impossible.")
Considering their hosts are friends of the poor, a voice for
liberty, not just of trade, scholars are truly startled and may

have to rethink their historical understanding of how to
promote economic and political equality without
compromising their moral and ethical concerns. In no manner

will the newcomers collude to corner the market, to raise
prices, and to deceive the public. (Bus shelters proclaim
their manifesto: "We do not, like Marinetti, 'intend to sing

the love of danger, the habit of energy and fearlessness.' All
we aspire to is a humane, decent and polite version of society.")
The officers are worried, "They're so small and delicate that

you'll mangle them when you're catching them." To avert untoward incidents, the Republic has deployed troops along the apartment hedges, as well as guards using tree branches to keep the residents in line.

1,000 cranes

Eastward, the folded paper cranes
sway from dim clouds,
the dream of peace and hope dangling
in the sweep of their plumage.
Mere rock, it seems, did not satisfy
the old, neither the unalterable
ancient pictographs in bone
drawn by time to convey ancestors' wishes,
paper being the ideal artifice
to record ideas, nor the long-necked birds
of heaven swooping out of the sky.
From a clod of hemp, bark, rags, fishnets
paper was first tamped to meet a Chinese calligrapher's
desire to write on something flat. Unparalleled,
the emptying of words
on a face that was both portable and replicable,
like a god holding
and withholding favours.

Offering

High on the valley's slopes the radar clocks
        the movements
of bear, deer, lynx, squirrel, and porcupine.
            Scrawny dogs track the decibel-distances
               of drones, ears to the ground,
there –
where the Northwest River
rives the yellow wooden houses near the shore,
           away from the white stucco houses
        dotting the hills dressed in wild pine.

     The children breathe in
        the vapour of memory:
           the earth, the water, the trees.
The barren ground caribou herd,
       the brook trout, the salmon
          call from a distance.
Snowmobiles rust near the shore.
      Golden apple berries ret in the marshes.
The wind erases notes on the massive rock faces.
         The children sing with the loping wolf
     howling into the firelight.

       At dawn,
upturned boats taunt their bottoms
       to the heaving sky,
the reeds and cattail
         flail their arms into the dark clouds.

I found the body heaving

"Only thin smoke without flame
From the heaps of couch-grass;
Yet this will go onward the same
Though dynasties pass."
– From "In Time of the Breaking of Nations" Thomas Hardy

I found the body heaving
while passively climbing, while
moving inside
the lines of famous and obscure
poems and failed experiments,
curiosities, overheard blather,
the idle thoughts of the eternal ones
who dream with a mirror and a dictionary,
their fractured imaginings twisted
round the windmill's halo, their memories
encrypted in understatement and plainness.
There was so much to be accomplished
while I made room for the body, the slant
of peculiar cadences and blur of birdcalls.
I had to hold back a hemorrhage of fear,
push the earth-carved cargo to the bone-
scarred battleground, craft shadow wings
from the carcass of craggy roots, a makeshift
prison out of the skull-toothed ridge.

Dream trilogy

1   The poetry teacher nudges us to write a line each
on the board. Whatever comes to mind, whatever
bothers us, in our workshop in the master's bedroom,
our clothes and sheets strewn on the bed, the stock
of sleep in our eyes. The man from Kabul digs a line,
our neighbour from Kandahar rills on his lamb stew,
our lines flow on the board like a banner, majestic hills float
in a drape of clouds, soaring cedars shelter
the air timorously. The gates of grace part our self-image,
project our self-fulfilling prophecy,
the tranquil languor of the land where two rivers meet.
The poet speaks in the voice of our ancestors
and all we remember is the last line: What is *is*,
our poem a dewdrop suspended at its tip. We urge
the poet to teach us to interpret dreams, cure sickness,
fall into trances, say what we believe – how not to break
the breath that makes us paint, carve stone and wood.
When life forces you into a corner, the river torrent will surge
like ink blacking out the tabloid warfare. We wake to fleeting
rain wetting the shaded tipica deep in the ravine.

2 My mother asks if the fruits are ripe yet, the vidalia
onions beet-violet as if they've signed up for Holy Week,
dressed as a garland to match Jesus' purple robe, before
he is crucified and crowned with thorns. Somewhere
in the Midwest, some farmer will be planting this crop,
one of a hundred hybrids to tease every mouth.
My mother frets only for her tree, never mind
if they bore onions and not apple pomes, never mind
if she's never seen apple trees nor tasted tarty onions.
Wanting to appease her, I pick a fruit dangling
from a submissive stem, the bulb as big as my fist,
offer it to the one who knows her onions,
only to feel it fall from no-one's hand, the broken skin tearing
juice, sweet salve unguing my interminable grief.

3   From the bedroom we run through the length and breadth of the house, a house that looks out into the trees and down the canyon, into the sea.

Our house is all windows, just how I dreamt it to be, for limning shadows of laurel and oak, shades of catalpa, the fortunes of squirrels gambling with whales in the moonlight as we watch a sperm whale dive a mile deep, hold its breath for an hour. Can we please have it? The dark centre of the flower-of-an-hour? We will leave you the flat line on the bed, lend us something to wear, give us back the folds of sleep, the crow's feet of memory, the man who stole fire, our old assumptions of the world.

A Cologne ago

I ate a plum a jackdaw pecked in Cologne,
on the royal steps from hell,
dividing my sins according to categories:
big and small, venial and mortal,
depending on the periodic table of occurrences,
hydrogen or helium, light as weightless atoms,
vulnerable as the flies from Patagonia. The row
of saints outside the cathedral smirked at me,
a ciphered tourist in my bag of clothes, aquiver
with my nothingness, lost in the keening
grey of old people's coats walking on the platz,
and burr of stationed sailors feeding pigeons
in an afternoon wrapped around the habits
of a common day. I wanted to go the distance,
break the minutes on the clock, account for my errors,
look in their eyes to find the eye of the one who once was,
who was us, among the flying buttresses,
the gargoyles singing a song without sound,
its shape mislaid in the stone tracery –

Rise

When no one else mourns, the virtual war
will be waged in new terrain, on chinked
photos of those killed by bombing raids.

Rise, the dead are nothing more than names
suggesting a common heritage, everything
except an audience, simulations of a million

configurations of things you didn't expect,
the unexplored plain conjuring deserts
of designed plats, mourners with damp eyes,

the coroner's morgue providing a framework
for infinite possibilities. From the matrix
of life a small steeple of stones, an imaginary

baby in its mother's arms, the cairn
of disbelief, the same tale of towns and villages.
They do not know what God is doing or where

He is looking, yet they want to appease
the other gods for their misdemeanours.
Their problem did not begin yesterday,

it is their destiny: finding splendour
in the shapes of shells, rhythm and perfume
in machine guns and poison gas.

Help them banish the error of old ways,
bring back the cave men who cared for the old,
infants with birth defects, unclaimed bodies,

unidentified persons, the unwanted,
the disappeared. After the third day, inscribe
their names in the book of life, bring them

to the morning island where conjugate auroras
dance around the earth.

Lift

1. Prolegomena: What the bird says

The bird wishes to say beforehand
(before you are absorbed by the sound
of the rapidly beating lath and strings of its wings),
that what is real is sometimes just supposition
and hearsay:
Flight is a catenoid unloosed, agitating arcs,
parabolas, gauzily pottering
in syncopated taps on tapered toe,
and round the wing – air's push and pull,
a spinning fan set to calibrate
soars and glides, lightness and stiffness.

2. Found

Found the bird knee-deep and exculpatory, embedded
in the man-made island paradise with its hunting grounds
now razed, and the tongueless smallmouth bass and carp
in a warren of lakes and canals taking the bait
as guards fly-fish near the army barracks.
In this summer of fitful waiting, Chinook fly,
black hawks hover high and low over the city's northern edge,
past the humming bees and recreant turret gunners.

3. The invasion of termites

Termites simmer in the trenches
as crows fly over, tracking the path of dogs
let loose in the hills. The king of the mountain forests
has confirmed that he would encourage and expect
the local chieftains to help remove the parasites
which threaten the enduring mountain passes
and the stability of his domain. He has also ordered
troop deployment in armoured carts to dig out
the militant termites while people wait
for what they have to say.

4. Last sighting

The hysterical pillage of the impoverished towns
is widely documented. The birds descended in circles
in a mane of brutal darkness, rotor blades ripping
easterly clouds, plundering hills in their relentless pursuit,
the birds of prey probing their theories of extinction,
the taxonomy of wounds and bruises of extirpation.
And soon they would be gone, bacteria and fungi
and megafauna, the bipedal species last sighted
retreating in the battered digestive tracts
of the mountains.

How they understood

They weep over what once was, linger.

Imagine first tenderness in everything,
how difficult the well of tears,
how impossible to think
it exists.
        Yet she remembers where
they turned beneath the sorrow
of places, when they stepped
on the flowers,
watched the little boy with his electronic
toy car,
how enthralled they were
with the omnipotence
of technology: the tumbling decoys,
the brightness and fluctuations
in brightness
of balloon-covered warheads
tumbling end-over-end.
        They've seen those lights
        once –
alpha, beta, gamma – pikadon
of thunder brighter than a thousand suns,
pure, blinding,
searing the back of a seven-fingered
island.

In her recollection, she finds it
unthinkable
        how they'd forgotten
they had once been concerned with
the simple
and the marvellous,
that the world around them spun
on a drop of water,
how they had once been vulnerable.

Restoration

I carried my sorrow onto the waiting road,
into the swiftly descending dusk,
past the tangle of shrubs and pine trees,

the jacinths unaware of the waning moon.
Rain, blind, followed wind, butting asphalt,
roofs, foliage, the neighbourhood of desires.

There were big drops, heavy as a restoration,
curved, diagonal, colliding, breaking up
into tiny droplets, like pulses skittering

down elevator chutes. There were inconsistent drops
falling unevenly like parts of the psyche,
floodmarks of inconstancy, doubled mirrors

on rain-backed tar after a spate of sightings.
If I could learn the language of their origin,
pin them down round and flat, like a safe stretch

of water in the drying patches,
I could perhaps play a dithyramb in the deepest hour
when complicity is distilled, let the past ride

its conditioned gestures.

Notes & Sources

1. "Beyond appearances"
This poem is a transposition of the poem "The Idea" by Mark Strand, which appeared originally in the June 12, 1989 issue of *The New Yorker* and was included in his book, *A Continuous Life*, published by Knopf, New York, 1997.

2. "1,000 cranes"
Based on Jon R. Luoma, "The magic of paper" *National Geographic*, Vol. 191, No. 3, p. 98 [88-109]. With permission by National Geographic.

3. "How they understood"
Inspired by an article, "What's Wrong with Missile Defense: An Interview with Ted Postol by Joshua Cohen," *Boston Review*, Vol. 26, No.5, October/November 2001, pp. 40-45. With permission by *Boston Review*.

4. Title Page Epigraph
The poem on the title page is from "The King of Asine" by George Seferis in *Four Greek Poets*, translated by Edmund Keeley and Philip Sherrard, Penguin Books, 1966, p. 58.

Glossary

Aba ginoong Maria, napupuno ka ng grasya (Pil.): Hail Mary, full of grace
abuela (Sp.): grandmother
antiquitaeten (Ger.): antiques
Ave Maria purisima (Pil.): Holy Mary...
banaba (Pil.): a tropical tree with butterfly-shaped leaves
bayan (Pil.): country
betel (Pil.): the fruit of the betel palm
britzka (Pol.): a wagon with a folding top
calamus: Asian palm, sweet flag, a reed
camias (Pil.): sour fruit used for stews and sweets
camisa chinos (Sp.) white cotton undershirts
catalpa: a hardy tree with large, heart-shaped leaves
frangipani: a tropical shrub or tree of the dogbane family with fragrant flowers
ikmo (Pil.): leaf from betel pepper family chewed with betel nut as a mild stimulant
Impermanencia, Lagarte (Sp.): not permanent, fleeting; lizard
jacinths: hyacinths
Jardin de la Flor (Sp.): flower garden
Jardin de la Nube (Sp.): snow garden
Jardin del Engano (Sp.): garden of enchantment
Jardin del Gusano (Sp.): silkworm garden
katuray (Pil.): a tropical tree with thin leaves, twigs and stems
Kumusta, Manong? (Pil.): derived from Spanish greeting, *Como esta, Senor?*: How are you, Sir?
kvas (Pol.): a fermented drink made from rye, barley
meron, wala, meron (Pil.): wealth/plenty, nothing, wealth/plenty
municipio (Sp.): municipal hall
nada (Sp.): nothing
nipa (Pil.): palm leaves used as roof and siding
pag-ibig sa tinubuang lupa (Pil.): love of country, homeland
pandesal (Pil.): bread bun, literally, bread of salt
panuelos (Sp.): scarves
patintero (Pil.): a game of catch, played in the open, with lines drawn from buckets of water
pitogo (Pil.): a palm tree
poblacion (Sp.): town square

salabat (Pil.): ginger tea
sampaguita (Pil.): a fragrant white flower from the jasmine family; the Philippines' national flower
Susmaryosep (Pil.): Jesus, Mary, Joseph!
tipica: a coffee tree
Tore ni David, toreng garing (Pil.): Tower of David, tower of ivory; from Litany prayer
un segundo, dos segundos (Sp.): one second, two seconds
Victoria Regia (Sp.): Queen Victoria
ylang-ylang (Pil.): a tropical tree bearing fragrant flower clusters